BLENDER 3D FOR BEGINNERS: THE COMPLETE GUIDE

The Complete Beginner's Guide to Getting Started with Navigating, Modeling, Animating, Texturing, Lighting, Compositing and Rendering within Blender.

Danan Thilakanathan

BLENDER 3D FOR BEGINNERS: THE COMPLETE GUIDE
Copyright © 2016 by Danan Thilakanathan.

Website:
http://www.thilakanathanstudios.com

This book is intended for the complete beginner of Blender as well as beginners in the world of 3D graphics and animation. This book aims to provide a starting point in all areas of Blender including navigation through Blender, modelling, texturing, lighting, animating, and so on.

I won't cover absolutely everything about Blender such as what each and every button does. This book would have to be the size of a dictionary if I attempted to explain everything. Instead, I will cover the bare basics and provide some easy follow-along exercises so that you can start to feel comfortable with Blender and give you confidence to jump in and do whatever you like with Blender. There is no tough jargon in this book, and any unfamiliar terminology will be explained to you in a simple and easy-to-understand manner.

I hope you find this book useful and hopefully make your journey to Blender mastery a smooth and enjoyable ride!

CONTENTS

CHAPTER ONE

Introduction

You are a complete beginner to the world of 3D modeling and/or animation and have decided upon Blender as your software tool of choice. First of all great choice! Second of all, you have found the right book! In this Complete Blender Beginner Guide, you will learn everything about getting started with Blender 3D! By the end of this book, you won't be able to make movies and games (these require separate skills). But you will at least be able to navigate your way around Blender hopefully as easily as navigating a car (assuming you know how to drive a car). You will learn everything from the Blender interface, to navigating the viewport, modeling, shading, lighting, sculpting, animating and so on! We'll cover a lot in this book but don't feel too overwhelmed. We will only be covering just the basics. You will find it most helpful to also follow along and try some of the stuff out instead of just reading. You tend to learn better (and faster) by trying things out physically instead of just memorizing random facts. Apart from learning, I hope you will also have some fun along the way!

Those shortcut keys tho…

One of the reasons why people may dislike Blender is that there are too many shortcut keys you have to remember. When I first started out, this is what mainly frustrated me. At the time, I'd rather memorize formulas from my High School Physics textbook as it seemed more worth it than memorizing shortcut keys for software that wasn't as popular at the time. Over time though, the shortcut keys stuck in my long-term memory after many Googling and reading those Blender guides. Blender has vastly improved from the older days though. Seriously. Working with Blender back then would almost be like learning to operate those buttons on a rocket-ship or something. Now, it's become a lot more intuitive. You don't need to memorize any shortcut keys anymore. There are intuitive buttons in the interface now that allow you to do pretty much everything. You can also search what you need by pressing the SPACE button. So knowing shortcut keys is no longer that important in Blender but obviously knowing them will help you speed up your workflow on whatever you're working on heaps.

I personally feel that Blender is perhaps the most powerful free 3D software in the world right now. No other software that I've seen can allow you to do everything from modeling, sculpting, animation, video editing, rendering and composition in the one software. And Blender does it really well! I think it's very possible that you can make your very own Shrek or Monsters Inc. with this thing! It's THAT powerful!

What to expect!

I've written this book in a way that it would be really easy-to-follow without any jargon. That is, you don't need to know anything about 3D and you should still be able to follow. I could have made video tutorials, but I've chosen to write a book instead since it may be more convenient for those who prefer to hide behind their laptops during class at school/college pretending to study.

If you follow along with the exercises in this book, you should be comfortable with Blender relatively quickly. Sometimes it may take more time, sometimes less. But don't get discouraged though and work at a pace that you feel most comfortable with. This isn't just another step-by-step Blender beginner tutorial, you can read this without even having Blender open (but trying out what you've learned will help you learn faster!)

Inspiration

Don't be fooled in thinking Blender is not as powerful or as good as other paid 3D software. Check out some of the awe-inspiring works created by other artists using Blender.

Figure 1. Landscape rendered in Blender Cycles by agus (BlendSwap)

Figure 2. A scene from Big Buck Bunny (c) copyright Blender Foundation | www.bigbuckbunny.org

Figure 3. A render from the BlenderGuru Architecture Academy Tutorial by monkeywing (Flickr)

Figure 4. German Country Road by David Gudelius

You won't learn how to make any of this in this book, but I leave it here just to show you the power of Blender and what you could potentially make with it. However, if you are persistent with Blender as well as learning about 3D art, you too can one day create art like this!

Get Blender!

If you don't have Blender installed already, it would be wise to go ahead and install it now. It shouldn't take too long (depending on your Internet speed of course). The steps to doing this are as follows:

1. Go to http://blender.org
2. Go to 'Download'.
3. Depending on what type of computer you have (Windows, Mac, Linux), select the right installer for you. I use Windows and just downloaded the direct .msi installer.
4. Follow the installation instructions and you should have Blender installed on your machine.

Summary

At this point, you should have Blender installed and ready to use. You should also (hopefully) be inspired and motivated enough to start learning about Blender! The next chapter focuses primarily on the Blender interface. It's important that you know the UI of Blender before you go and make anything. Just like when you learned to first drive. Your first lesson would likely have been to know where the steering wheel is, where the break and the accelerator is and so on.

CHAPTER TWO

The Blender Interface

Before we go and make any 3D related stuff like movies, we need to first take some time to understand the Blender interface. At first glance, you'll probably notice that the interface doesn't look like those Windows applications. Nor does it look like any application from Apple, Android, or any other OS for that matter. It's sort of unique in a way. Once you get a hang of the almighty Blender interface, you'll feel like you're in full control as an artist/animator/game designer/etc. By the end of this chapter, you will have a better understanding of and be able to customize your own Blender interface.

So let's get into it! First things first, Blender is made up of pretty much windows. For example, you might have Google Chrome open in one window and Microsoft Word open in another. Maybe you'll have Media Player running in another window. Blender functions in a similar way!

You might have the 3D view open in one window, a video editor open in another and an image editor open in another. In Blender, these so-called 'apps' are called Editors. You can create as much windows as you want in Blender and change the Editor within each window. Hopefully this makes sense?

Figure 5. Here are all the available editors in Blender

Explain the interface already…

If the window thing doesn't make sense, let me start right at the beginning and describe the first thing that shows when you open Blender. You'll probably see the Blender splash logo. You can click out of that. The below image is what you should see when you open Blender. This is the default Blender interface.

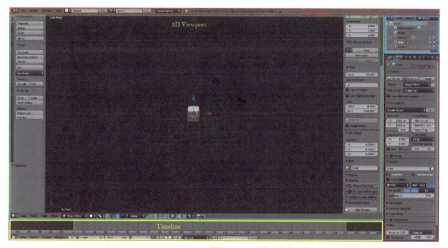

Figure 6. The Blender Interface

If you don't see this screen, you've probably downloaded some other software by mistake. http://blender.org should be the legitimate website! That, or you've probably come across this book this sometime in the future at which point Blender might have changed to a brand new interface.

See where I've highlighted boxes everywhere. Yes, these are examples of windows in Blender. Within each window are Editors (3D Viewport, Timeline, Properties, etc.). Before I go further, let me give you a very brief description of the Editors you see in the above Blender interface.

Green Box – This is the 3D viewport. Here is where you will make your 3D animated movie. You create 3D models here, you animate them here, you see them come to life here. This is one of the most important editors in Blender. It would be pretty difficult (and dead silly) to animate or model something without the 3D viewport open. See the buttons you see on the right? This is the toolbar and contains a lot of the functionality that you would previously had to remember some shortcut key for. Pretty handy!

Blue Box – This the Outliner. Every 3D object you have in your 3D viewport (including objects, lights and cameras) will be visible as a list here. This is useful if you have so many 3D objects in your scene and want to find the exact object by just searching. Say you're working on a massive epic scene involving thousands of soldiers for example. You might struggle to find the soldier named "Bob" in the 3D viewport alone. In the Outliner, you can search by typing "Bob" and the list will filter to show that soldier. On a side note, I cannot picture a soldier with a name of Bob. It just doesn't sound powerful for some reason.

Maroon Box – The Properties editor. This is pretty much the jam in the toast (Sorry, that's the best I could come up with. It sounded better in my head though). This editor pretty much sets up the properties for most of Blender. If you want to render, you will need to come here. If you need to add materials to your models, you need to come here. If you want to add hair, fluids or other physics, you would come here as well. If you want to add some advanced camera effects like depth-of-field or motion blur, you will need to come here. If you want to make changes to your 3D world such as dimensions, you will still need to come here. It's one of the most important editors in Blender just like the 3D viewport. In some cases it's more important than the 3D viewport. Take video editing for example, you don't even need the 3D viewport open at all but you still need Properties when you do your final render!

Yellow Box – The Timeline. You can playback your animation here, set start and end times of your animations and other timeline related stuff like adding markers. Not much else to say, it's pretty straightforward.

Red Box – This is Info editor. You have a File menu where you can do stuff like Save, Open, New, Preferences, etc. Then there's the Render menu which contains options to render images or animations. The Window menu allows you to select whether you want to work full screen or create a screenshot of your scene. The Help menu gives you options for help (I guess that would be obvious, lol). Next, you have the screen-layout dropdown menu thing (A bit of detail on this below). Next to this, you'll find the Scene selection dropdown. This allows you to create several scenes in Blender file. For example, you could animate 2 friends having a phone conversation. One friend could be at home and the other friend could be in a different country or just hopping off the train or something. You could create 2 different Scenes in Blender and then join them together in the video editor. Next to the Scene selection dropdown, is your current Blender version (yours is likely to be higher than mine) and information about your scene such as the total amount of vertices/faces, how much memory your scene is consuming and your currently selected object.

Screen Layouts

Now back to the screen-layout dropdown that I mentioned a few sentences ago. When you click the dropdown, you see this:

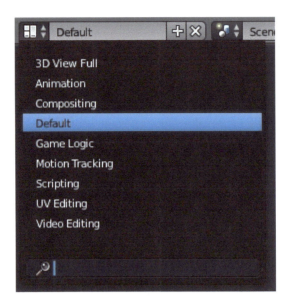

In this dropdown, you see a bunch of different options such as Animation, Compositing and Game Logic. Clicking them will take you to a different looking layout of Blender. This doesn't mean Blender has switched to some different state. It's still the same Blender but with different windows containing different Editors. For example, clicking Animation will take you to a layout containing the most optimal editors you would need for animation. Clicking Video Editing will get rid of the 3D viewport (that's not necessary as you only work with already made video, images and music). Instead, it shows editors that are related to video editing.

If you don't like the layouts shown here or want more different layouts, you can create your own layout! You have the ability to create your own Blender interface! You just have to press the plus '+' button next that you see there. This will duplicate the current layout. So if I'm already in Default layout. Pressing the '+' button will create a Default.001 which is a clone. You can then modify this layout to suit your needs.

Another thing! You can change the size of your windows by dragging any edge of a window up or down (shown in black arrows). You can create more windows by dragging the 3 diagonal line thingies (shown in red) away. This makes the Blender interface oh-so customizable!

Summary

That's it for now I guess! In this chapter, you learnt about windows, the main parts of the Blender interface and screen layouts. Spend some more time playing around with the Blender interface and try to get comfortable with it! You will see for yourself just how flexible and customizable it is! In the next chapter, we will focus on one window: The Properties window. Remember how I mentioned this was the jam in the toast. If you know a bit about the properties window, you can do all sorts of stuff with Blender and start to feel a sense of comfort and control of Blender overall.

13

CHAPTER THREE

The Properties Panel

In the previous chapter, you learnt about the Blender Interface! I had touched on a bit about the Properties window. Since it is one of the most important features of Blender, I will be giving a brief overview of the Blender Property panel. By the end of this chapter, you will have an understanding of the Property window and hopefully gain more confidence using this software!

Below is what you should see at the top of the Property panel.

As you can see, there are all these different buttons. Some of them look somewhat obvious at first glance, others look pretty confusing (or maybe even disturbing to some but hopefully not). I will now step through one-by-one with each button and explain what they do!

First, the **Render** settings. This is where you go when you want to render an image or animation. You can set the location where you want to store your rendered stuff. You can also adjust a bunch of values here that will give you the best quality renders for your scene. Apart from test renders, you would generally come here once you're scene is ready with the lights and cameras in place. The result is usually satisfaction from a beautiful render or tears realizing how much more you need to learn.

This is the **RenderLayer** settings. This allows you to set up which layers you want to render. For example, you might have objects in your scene that you don't want to be seen in a render. You can put those objects in a separate renderlayer and hide them during render time. You can also add and combine more than one render layer. This is most beneficial for artists who may want to work with each element in their scene individually during compositing or something.

In the **Scene** settings, you set up your 3D world. You can change from the default Blender unit system to the real-world metric system (the one with centimetres and metres). You can also set the gravity of your 3D world. The default is -9.8m/s/s. This is the real value that keeps us grounded on Earth. The negative value means we are being shoved towards the ground. A positive value will make us fly towards the sky. If you change the value to 0, you would simulate space. Good if you're

15

making a space movie like "Gravity"!

The **World** settings allow you to define what your sky will look like. Whether you want daytime, nigh time, cloudy or extra-terrestrial, you light up your sky here.

This is the **Object** settings. This allows you to modify the current object that is selected in the 3D viewport. You can change things like location, rotation and scale. You can also change the name of the object, how it should be displayed in the viewport, whether it should be visible. Pretty powerful object manipulation here!

The **Constraints** tab allows you to create one or more constraints for your currently selected 3D object. You get to set laws for your objects and they have to obey! Power to the artist! You can make your object follow a path, or copy the movements of another object. You can make another object "stick" to another object. Like a hat being "stuck" on a person's head. You can also make an object point at another object. For instance, you can make your camera point at your character no matter where he/she moves! You can really reduce the time needed to animate everything. Pretty cool stuff I reckon!

This is the **Modifiers** settings. A modifier is used to transform your object without destroying the original model in any way. There are loads of modifiers in Blender. With modifiers, you can explode your objects, bend them, and do all sorts of things with them. If you remove (or hide) the modifier, your original model still remains intact.

This is the **Object Data** settings. This adds properties to your currently selected object in Edit Mode. You mainly visit this tab to set Vertex Groups and/or shape keys.

The **Materials** tab is where you create shaders for your 3D objects. You can define a very basic shader for your object here. With the Cycles render engine, you have the ability to create even more advanced shaders (like realistic human skin or translucent leaves for example) but you would need to go to the Node Editor (yet another Editor) to customize your shaders. With Blender Internal, you can pretty much create most of your shaders within the Materials tab.

The **Texture** tab allows you to import your own image textures or use some of the procedural textures built into Blender. There are variety of different procedural textures within Blender with the most popular one being the Cloud texture. This tab isn't only for Materials but can also be used for sculpting brushes or defining a normal/displacement map (images that creates bumps on your object, but you don't need to know what these are for now if you're completely new to all this).

The **Particle** settings allow you to create fur/hair/hairy stuff that emit from your 3D object. You can add hair to your character or add fur to your dog. I'm guessing this would be obvious, lol. Alternatively, you also come here if you want to generate particles emitting from your 3D object. Particles are great for fireworks or rain for example.

The last tab (phew) is the **Physics** tab. Here you can simulate real-world physics. You can make cloth animation here. You can make water/fluid animation. You can make wind effects. You can also make stuff crash and collide with each other. You would visit this tab a lot if you were working on an epic car crash scene!

Summary

And that's all the modifiers! Wow, that was a lot of tabs! In this chapter, you looked at all the tabs in the Properties window and started to gain an understanding of how to do some awesome stuff with Blender. It may feel like it's a little bit too much to take in right but it's not that many when you look at it in Blender. In the next chapter, we will learn about navigating our way through Blender. So doing things like moving around the viewport, messing around with 3D objects, and some useful shortcut keys to make your life easier.

CHAPTER FOUR

Navigating through Blender

So far, we have learnt a bit about how Blender is structured and what each component does. It's pretty awesome to know that Blender is powerful and all, but it's now time to go ahead and learn to actually **use** Blender. By the end of this chapter, you will have learnt the main essentials of Blender navigation. I won't show you all the navigation keys because there would be too many to list so I'll just keep it to the most important ones.

The 3D "world" in Blender is made up of 3 axes (X-axis, Y-axis and Z-axis). If you look in the bottom left-hand corner of the 3D viewport, you will see a red, green and blue thingy with XYZ letters on them. These are the axes. The blue axis represents the Z-axis, the red axis represents the X-axis and the green represents the Y-axis. Your 3D object is mapped to a coordinate (X,Y,Z) on these axes. So for example, the default cube is at

(0,0,0) meaning it is at the origin (or center) of the 3D axes. An object at (3,0,0) means the object is at the center but 3 places to the left of the X-axis.

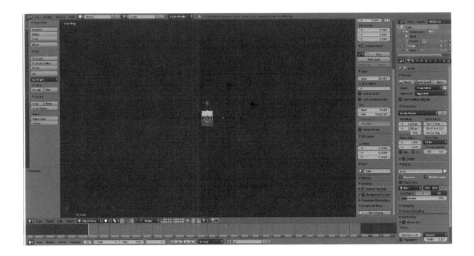

Selecting Objects

To select an object (like the default cube), you just have to hover your mouse over the object and *right-click*.

To select a few objects at a time, you can either circle select or box select. To circle select, press *C* and then scroll in-out to get the circle size you want. Once you're happy, left click and drag around to select the objects you want. This should feel like painting a little bit. Once you're done selecting, right-click again. To box select, press *B* (you'll see a grey square looking thing which follows your mouse everywhere it goes), then *left-click* and drag until you've covered all the objects you want selected. To de-select objects, use the same method with circle select or box select, but instead of left clicking, do *middle-mouse click* instead. (Another way of selecting is using the lasso tool. You can do this by *Ctrl + left click* dragging around your objects. This method isn't that popular, though it can be useful to some. Just thought I'd put this out there.)

To select all the objects in your scene, simply press *A* (Make sure your mouse is in the 3D viewport and not somewhere else like the Timeline for example). You can also de-select all the objects in your scene by pressing *A* again.

Transforming Objects

There are 3 ways to transform an object. You can *move* an object, *rotate* an object, and *scale* an object. By the way, cameras and lights cannot be scaled in Blender.

To *move* an object, first make sure your object is selected (by ***right-clicking***) and then press *G* and move anywhere to your heart's desire. To rotate an object, press *R* and then rotate the selected object anywhere. To scale an object, press *S* and then move the mouse in and out and see your selected object grow and shrink. Press ***Enter*** once you're happy with your transformation.

You can do a bit more than that. Like in our example above, if you want to move the object 3 places to the left of the X-axis, just press *G* and then *X*. Now you can only move along the X-axis. To get exactly 3 places to the left, just press *3* and then hit ***Enter***.

NOTE: You can also click on the colored arrows (which represent each axis) that are visible on the selected object and drag to move along the axes.

Modifying the View

Cool, we know how to do some basic stuff with 3D objects in Blender. Now let's learn some basic stuff about navigating the 3D viewport.

To rotate around the 3D viewport, just middle-click and drag anywhere. To zoom-in and out, just scroll in and out (*Ctrl + middle click* dragging also does the same thing). To move your viewport, press Shift and then middle-click and drag.

Let me recap that:

Rotate viewport – *Middle-click + drag*.

Zoom in and out – *Scroll in and out*.

Move around – *Shift + middle-click drag*.

You can also navigate via the numpad on your keyboard. Here's a summary:

Numpad 7	Numpad 8	Numpad 9
Top View	Rotates upwards	Rotates to opposite view
Numpad 4	**Numpad 5**	**Numpad 6**
Rotates rightwards	Orthogonal View	Rotates leftwards
Numpad 1	**Numpad 2**	**Numpad 3**
Front View	Rotate downwards	Left View

Pressing Shift + 1, 3 or 7 will give you the opposite view. In other words,

Shift+ Numpad 1 – Back view

Shift + Numpad 3 – Right view.

Shift + Numpad 7 – Bottom view.

Since we're talking about the numpad, I'll show you what the other keys do as well.

Numpad + - Zooms in.

Numpad - - Zooms out.

Numpad . - Sets whatever 3D object you selected to be the main pivot point for rotation.

Numpad / - View the selected 3D object locally. In other words, all other objects in the scene will temporarily disappear until you press Numpad / again. This is useful if you're working on a heavy cluttered scene, and want to concentrate on one 3D object without the other objects getting in the way.

Toolbars

To do some awesome modeling stuff in Blender, you can use the toolbar. Pressing *N* and/or *T* will open up toolbars on either side depending on which one you pressed. Press them again to hide them. As a short exercise, open up the right-toolbar (pressing *N*) and then move an object like a cube (using *G*). Observe the top panel called 'Transform'. You will see these values being changed as you move your object. You can also type in here directly. Type *3* in the X box. Like in our example earlier, this should move the object 3 places to the left of the X-axis.

Don't know the right shortcut key?

Most of these shortcut key functionality can be done by pressing the right corresponding button somewhere within Blender. For example, with the numpad view switching above, you can do the same thing by going to the View menu in the 3D viewport and changing the view there.

If there's some other functionality you want to carry out but don't know how and where to look, you can search it. In fact, the following may just be the most important shortcut key to remember. Press ***Ctrl+A*** to find any functionality you want.

Or, you can go to here:

http://thilakanathanstudios.com/2015/09/blender-keyboard-shortcuts/

Download the infographic, print it out and stick it on your wall or something. That way, if you ever forget what you want to do, you can refer to the infographic quickly and easily.

Summary

In this chapter, we learnt about ways to navigate around Blender. We looked at ways to navigate the 3D viewport and do some cool things with 3D objects like *moving*, *rotating* and *scaling* them. Take time to learn these and try out the stuff in this chapter. Once you are comfortable with the basics of Blender navigation, you will begin to feel confident of mastering Blender! In the next chapter, we will finally start doing exciting stuff with Blender: 3D modelling!

CHAPTER FIVE

3D Modeling Basics

In this chapter, we will learn the basics of 3D modeling in Blender! By the end of this chapter, you will be able to do some basic modeling in Blender!

Modeling in Blender is generally quite fast (even faster with shortcut keys) and fun to work with. When you open Blender initially, you will be presented with the default cube which should already be selected (if not, select it).

You will notice at the bottom of the 3D window that you are in 'Object Mode'. This means you are currently working on your 3D object at the general object level (if that makes sense). You can't do any actual modeling with it whatsoever. If you want to go in and model and stuff your 3D object up, you need to be in 'Edit Mode'. This mode will show you all the vertices, edges and faces that you can pull, stretch, bend and twist to your desires. So, if you want to model an object, select your object (by **right-clicking**) and go to *Edit Mode*!

Easy shortcut key tip: You can also go to *Edit Mode* by pressing ***Tab***.

Vertices, Edges and Faces

In Blender, a 3D object is made up of vertices, faces and edges. Vertices are those dots. Edges are those lines and can have 2 or more vertices at its endpoints. Faces are the actual surface of your 3D object. We'll only work with vertices in this tutorial. If you want to do the same kind of stuff with edges or faces, just change the selection mode at the bottom of the 3D window as shown below.

In other words,

> To work with <u>vertices</u>, you would click the Vertex Select Mode.
> To work with <u>edges</u>, you would click the Edge Select Mode.
> To work with <u>faces</u>, you would click the Face Select Mode.

Messing up your 3D object

Now we are ready to do some basic modeling in Blender. Let's start easy! You can select any vertice by *right-clicking*. You can also select multiple vertices if you want by either *Shift+right-click*, or doing a box-select (*B + left-click drag*) or circle-select (*C + left-click*. Then *ESC* to finish selection). You can also select all the vertices by pressing *A*. Pressing *A* again will de-select all vertices.

Then you can do modify your object in any way you want. You can use the same shortcut keys as I showed in this tutorial here! Select any vertice by *right-clicking* and move and/or rotate them by hitting *G* and/or *R* respectively. We can't scale a single vertice as that wouldn't make any sense. You can however, scale if you have multiple vertices selected. To do this, just select a bunch of vertices (or even just 2 vertices) and then press *S*.

Modeling Tools

Of course, modeling in Blender is more than just pushing and pulling random vertices and faces. The 2 most used modeling tools in Blender (at least for me) is the Loop Cut tool and the Extrude tool!

Loop Cuts

Loop cuts can add better details to your 3D models and help shape the object to exactly the way you want it. To add a loop cut, hover your mouse somewhere on your 3D object, then press *Ctrl+R*. Blender will show you a purple line that sort of "wraps" around your 3D object. This is where Blender shows you where you are about to add a loop. If you like this position, then left-click. This will put a new loop around your 3D object and give you some more vertices, edges and faces to play with. If you haven't left-clicked yet, you can *scroll **up*** and/or ***down*** to get more loop cuts in the same area.

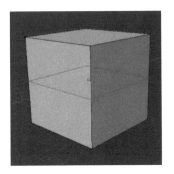 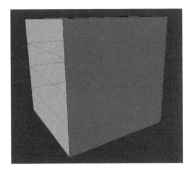

Extrusion

Extrusion is like forcing out more of a surface on your already existing mesh surface. It might make more sense if you try it out for yourself.

Go to *Face Select Mode* and select any random face. Then extrude out that face by pressing **E** and then moving your mouse up (or down). You should have forced a new set of vertices, edges and faces. You can do all sorts of stuff with Extrude! Most 3D models you create will mostly likely start from a simple shape and then will need a few extrusions to get the base shape of the 3D model you want to create. A lot of those YouTube "modeling in Blender" tutorials will use extrusion a lot!

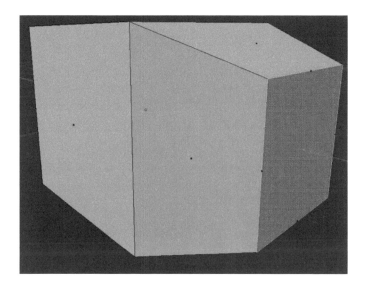

Modifiers

Modifiers are operations you can carry out on your 3D object in a non-destructive manner. There are a lot of different modifiers you can choose in Blender and each of them does a pretty cool thing. Modifiers can save a lot of time, especially since you don't have to do as much modeling in Blender.

The one that's heavily used though is the *Subdivision Surface Modifier* (or *SubSurf* for short). When modeling in Blender, you might get too sharp and jagged edges. SubSurf will smooth everything out and making it higher detailed. The smoothing out will generally get rid of sharp edges and is thus most effective for organic type of models like characters, animals or magical creatures.

Figure 7. Full list of modifiers in Blender

Curves

Another cool way of modelling in Blender is by using *curves*! There are a lot of objects that have curvature to them in real life. A rollercoaster for example, or a wine glass, a coke bottle, antique furniture items and so on. You could model them by hand, but a nice quicker way would be to make use of curves in Blender.

To add a curve in Blender, just go ***Shift+A → Curve → Bezier***. You'll see options other than Bezier, and any of them would be alright, but I choose Bezier because it's simple enough to start off with.

Once you've added the curve, you can modify it by going into Edit Mode and doing the same transforms as with any other objects. First, you would ***Tab*** into Edit Mode. You can then select any point(s) by ***right-clicking*** and do the usual move (by pressing ***G***), rotating (by pressing ***R***) and scaling (by pressing ***S***). You can also make your curve even longer by selecting a point and then pressing ***E***.

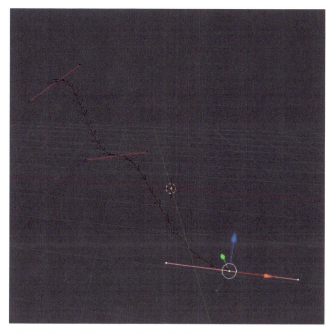

If you've done 3D modeling before, you may have heard of a technique of creating wine glasses from a curve. That is, using a curve, the tool will spin the curve around to create a wine glass shape. To do this in Blender, first create your curve and outline the shape you want. Then, go to the Modifiers, and add a *Screw* modifier. You should now have a wine glass type of shape. If you don't, you may need to change your axes in the *Screw* modifier settings.

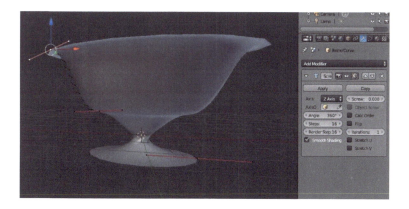

You can also give your curves some thickness by going to the Object Data panel in the Properties Window and changing the *Fill* to "Full". Then set the Bevel *Depth* to a thickness that you want. You can also bump up the Bevel *Resolution* so that it looks smoother.

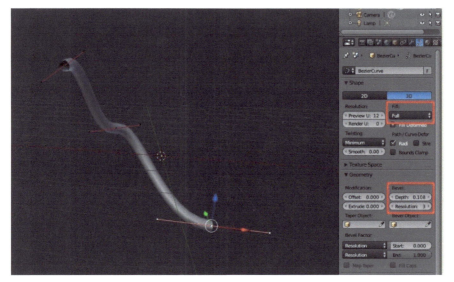

Summary

So that's the very basics of modeling in Blender. In this chapter, you've learnt the extreme basics of modelling in Blender. There are tons of good quality "modeling in Blender" tutorials out there on the Internet. Well now you know the extreme basics, I guess you should be able to start following those YouTube tutorials now! You are now able! In the next chapter, we will learn about creating shaders for our 3D objects so that it will look the way we want it when rendered.

CHAPTER SIX

Creating Shaders for your 3D objects

In this chapter, I will give a brief introduction to the Blender Shaders system! This is mainly a Blender Cycles Tutorial and by the end of this chapter, you will know how to create shaders for your own 3D objects in Blender so that it will look awesome when rendered!

First thing first, I need to let you know this will be a Blender Cycles tutorial. So make sure you are working with the Cycles render engine. At the top menu, if it says "Blender render", click the dropdown and change it to "Cycle Render". Blender Internal rendering seems to be phasing out so it seems fitting to learn about Cycles.

The main advantage of Cycles is that it can give you photo-realistic results compared to BI and setting up complex shaders is far simpler. The disadvantage however, is slower render times (but I learn that it is getting better).

The image below shows just how powerful Cycles really is:

Figure 8. An image I made with Blender Cycles

That's my own image above and I don't really specialize in photorealistic rendering. I just worked with the default shaders without much complex shader setup. In fact, there are even better examples and one simply has to do a Google Image search to see the awesome renders by the Blender community!

With Blender Cycles, you have the ability to create complex shaders for your 3D models. A complex shader setup is mainly needed if you want to simulate realistic human skin or grungy type materials. Photorealistic images tend to use complex shader setups.

With Cycles, you mainly use nodes to define your shader. This is what the nodes of a complex shader looks like:

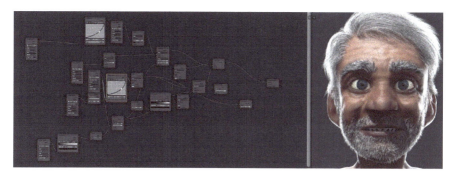

Figure 9. Skin shader node setup for characters in "Uyir"

It looks so complex but once you get the hang of it, you will realize how dead easy it really is. Blender could have made the nodes look cleaner and more intuitive (like BI) but personally, I like it the way it is. Mainly because when people pass me by, they think I'm working on something important. Like I'm an important researcher working on an important science or even a rocket application.

Let's learn by example!

Open up Blender and make sure your default cube is selected.

Now let's add a shader to our cube. To do this, go to the Property Panel, and select the *Material* tab. If there is no material there, just press the + sign to create a new one.

Here we can start to create our shader. Press "Use Nodes". And also, make sure you can see a Preview of your material which is probably above the "Use Nodes" button.

Cool! We can now work with creating a shader using nodes for our cube model.

Change your *3D viewport* editor to the *Node Editor*. You should see the default node setup for the cube. It is a diffuse shader node connected to the *Material Output* node. The *Material Output* node is pretty obvious in what it does. It takes whatever shader that's connected to the *Surface* input and displays it on your 3D object. If you use volumetric shaders, you use the Volume input and if you want to add things like bumps to your models, you use Displacement. That's pretty much how the node system works. It takes inputs from other nodes, processes them somehow and outputs the result to another node until it eventually reaches the output node.

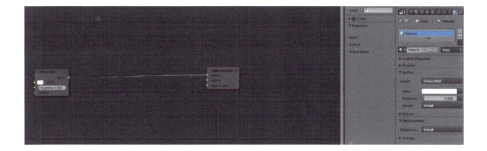

Blender Shaders

There are so many different shaders in Blender and you can add them by **Shift+A → Shader** in the Node Editor and select the shader you want. Here is a summary of the main shaders in Blender Cycles.

- *Diffuse Shader* – The default shader in Blender Cycles. It takes a color input and just displays it as it is. You can select any color you want or you could input an actual image texture.

- *Glossy Shader* – Makes your objects shiny and reflective. A roughness of 0 will give you a mirror and higher than that will give you blurry reflections.

- *Glass Shader* – Makes your 3D object see-throughable (if that's a word) like glass. Higher roughness values will give you blurrier glass.

- *Transparent Shader* – Makes your object invisible. You can control the opacity using image textures.

- *Translucency Shader* – The lights will penetrate through your 3D object and the back of your 3D object where there is no light will be partially lit up. Great for leaves, grass and ears!

- *Subsurface Scattering* – Makes your 3D object look like skin. Great for human skin, jelly, milk, and other gooey kind of stuff!
- *Velvet Shader* – Gives you a cloth like shader.
- *Mix Shader* – Mixes 2 different shaders together.
- *Add Shader* – Adds both shaders together.

Let's make paint!

So with this knowledge let's make a simple shiny paint like shader.

In the Node Editor, add a glossy shader by *Shift+A* -> *Shaders* -> *Glossy BSDF*. Alternatively, you can do *Add* -> *Shaders* -> *Glossy BSDF*.

Now do the same thing above but this time, make sure it's the *Mix Shader*.

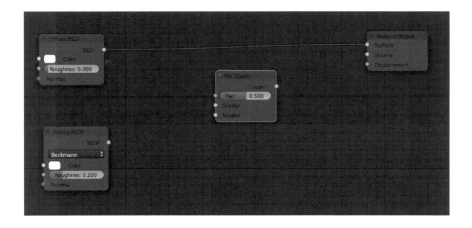

Connect the *Diffuse* and *Glossy shader* outputs to one of the input shader dots on the *Mix Shader*. To connect nodes, you just left-click and drag from one of the little circles to another little circle. You can also connect by selecting 2 nodes (e.g., right-clicking *Diffuse* and then **Shift+right-clicking** *Mix Shader*), and then pressing **F**.

Finally, connect the *Mix Shader* output to the *Material Output* Surface. In the preview window you should see your new material output.

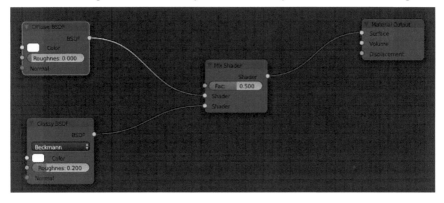

To make it look like paint a bit more, turn the roughness value of the *Glossy* down to 0.05 or so.

We need more *Diffuse* and less *Glossy* to make it look like paint. You do this by changing the Fac (or Factor) value in the *Mix Shader*. This controls the proportion of the shader's effect. Change the Fac value in the *Mix Shader* depending on where you placed the *Diffuse*. In other words if you placed the *Diffuse* above the *Glossy*, move the Fac value down to 0.1 or so. If you placed the *Diffuse* below the *Glossy*, move the Fac value up to 0.9 or so. Either way, what we're trying to do is get 10% *Glossy* and 90% *Diffuse*.

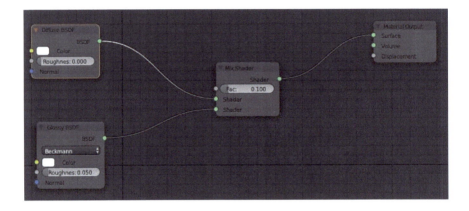

Look at your preview shader, it should look something like shiny paint now.

You can go a step further and play around with the colors. You can also add image textures if you want. To add images, just do *Shift+A* → *Texture* → *Image Texture*. Fire up your image and then connect the output to any shader input.

Summary

In this chapter, you learnt about Blender Cycles shaders and creating a simple car paint shader. You now have some idea of how shaders work in Blender Cycles. Play around with these shaders, go crazy, render them out and see how it looks. Try out some tutorials on YouTube to learn how to do some really advanced stuff. I can't guarantee you will be able to create advanced shaders like human skin or grungy metal but there are tutorials on YouTube that will teach you that sort of thing. The longer you play around with shaders, the more comfortable you will become working with them and the better you shaders will become. In the next chapter, we will learn how to do texturing in Blender. So all that stuff about UV maps and seams and that kind of stuff. A good understanding of texturing can also help you deliver more realistic and beautiful renders.

CHAPTER SEVEN

Texturing

In this chapter, you will learn how to do basic UV unwrapping and texturing in Blender. You don't need to know anything about UV or mapping to follow this chapter. Btw, UV has nothing to do with sun rays.

The Theory Stuff

Before we get to Blender UV mapping and what it is, we need to know a bit about texturing. In the previous post, we learnt how to create Cycles shaders. Creating plain default shaders for your 3D models sure isn't fun. You would have played around with different colors for your diffuse shaders, glossy shaders, or whatever to make it look more interesting. Apart from just changing colors, you can use textures. In the Node Editor, if you press *Shift+A* ➔ *Textures*, you will be presented with a few different texture types. These should be really obvious what they do.

For example, if you choose *Brick Texture*, then you will get a brick like texture on your 3D models. If you select *Noise Texture* then you will get this colorful cloudy type of texture (Ok, that probably wasn't as obvious, lol). These textures are called Procedural Textures (except the *Image Texture*). In other words, these textures will look good and consistent from any angle (as long as you set it up right). Procedural Textures are basically computer-generated textures.

However, sometimes you just don't want that procedural look. Adding image textures instead of procedural textures tend to make your 3D models look a lot more appealing and just well, better. If you're aiming for photorealism in your renders, you would certainly need to use real-world image textures a lot in your 3D models. The below image shows a procedural brick texture (left) and a real-world image texture of a brick (right) applied to a mesh. Clearly, the real-world image texture will look better on your 3D models than the procedural one.

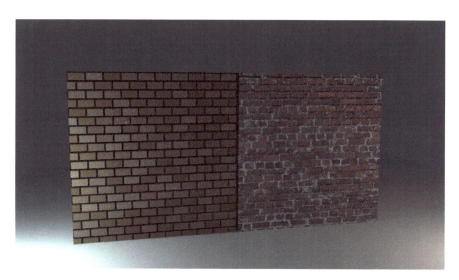

Figure 10. Procedural (left) and Image (right) textures

But how do you define where the image texture maps to your 3D models. What I mean is, say you're working on this really bad and buff 3D dude. And you want to add a tattoo on his arm. Firstly, procedural textures won't cut it. A computer cannot generate a tattoo. Actually, it might if you use some complex algorithm but what I mean is, you probably want to design the tattoo yourself using Photoshop or GIMP or something. Secondly, it will be difficult to tell the computer to put the tattoo specifically on the arm and nowhere else. Procedural textures tend to distribute the texture all over the model.

So if you want to define (or paint) your 3D models, you need to use image textures. But how would you map the image of the tattoo to the buff dude's arm? It's not like Blender's thinking "Oh yep, this is a tattoo image, so let's stick it on this dude's arm and hope my master approves". You would need to do this mapping by yourself. This process is called *UV unwrapping* in Blender. The idea is that the vertices, faces and edges (coordinates) will be arranged in a 2D mapping grid. When you place your own image on top of the 2D grid, the coordinates in the grid containing the image will copy over the image to the corresponding coordinates on the 3D model. That was a bit difficult to explain. Here is a simpler explanation. Think of it like your 3D object wearing a full body suit. That suit is then squashed and arranged in a way that you can paint on it like a canvas. Sometimes you would cut pieces of the suit that are a bit difficult to paint on and put it on another vacant part of the canvas.

Blender UV Mapping Types

There are various types of Blender UV mapping options available. To see them, select your 3D model, tab into Edit Mode, make sure all vertices are selected and press *U*. The ones you would most likely be using throughout your Blender life is *Unwrapping, Smart UV Project* and *Project from View*.

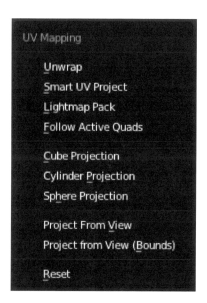

- *Project From View* – Perhaps the easiest form of UV unwrapping for beginners. Based on whatever view you are currently in the 3D viewport (front, side, or on an angle), the selected vertices will be "snapshot" onto the map. In other words, where you stand when you see the body suit, you take a picture, lay the photo down and paint on top of it. This method is perfect for tables and buildings and other cube-like objects.

- *Smart UV Project* – The computer chooses the most optimum mapping based on the selected vertices.

- *Unwrap* – Great for precise and correct UV mapping. This is what is mainly used in industry and as an artist you are mainly in control of the texturing. You mainly see this method being used for character texturing. This works by first letting you, the artist, define seams. Then those seams are "cut" and arranged on the "canvas" in a way that is ready to paint.

Learn by Example!

Enough of the boring theory stuff. Let's learn by example. Blender UV mapping is a lot simpler to actually do than to explain.

(1) Open up Blender and select your default cube.

(2) Drag out a new window and change the type to *UV/Image Editor*. Also, drag out another window and change type to *Node Editor*. (Remember: To drag out a new window, left-click the corner of the window where you see the 3 diagonal lines and drag out).

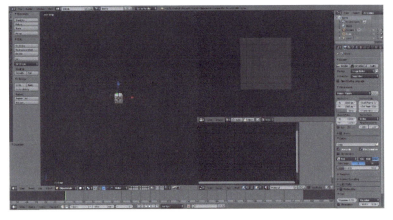

(3) In the 3D viewport, tab into Edit Mode and select all vertices. Pressing *A* will select/de-select all vertices.

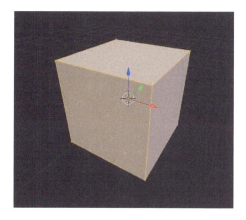

(4) Now press **U** to Unwrap and select 'Unwrap' as the option. (Menu version: ***Mesh -> UV Unwrap -> Unwrap***).

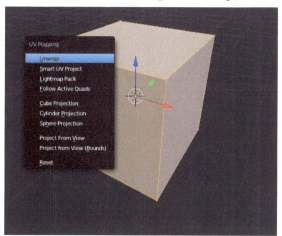

(5) Observe the *UV/Image Editor* and see your 2D map. You should see a large square. Actually this is all the faces of the cube superimposed on top of one another. You can test this by selecting some of the vertices and moving them around. It unwraps this way because Blender doesn't really know how to layout the UV map and makes an attempt at it anyway.

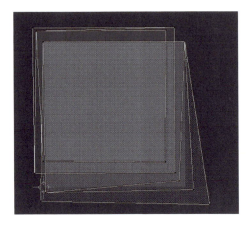

(6) Now change to the *Edge Select* mode.

(7) So now we'll add seams. This is like telling Blender to cut the mesh using scissors so it will be easy to "unfold" and layout in the UV map. So let's do that! Select all vertices by pressing *A* (if not done already), then press ***Ctrl+E***. This opens open a menu containing a bunch of stuff you can do with the edges. Another way is to go ***Mesh -> Edges***. Then press ***Mark Seam***. You will see all the edges of your cube turn red. This now means every edge in your cube has seams marked and Blender will cut every edge.

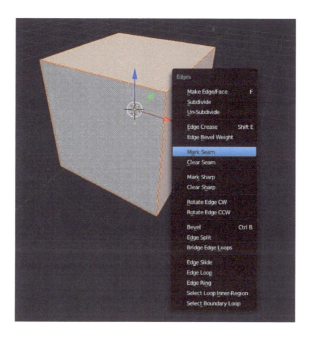

(8) Unwrap again and see the result. It seems it has unwrapped nicely but it really hasn't. If you select any vertice on the map and move it around, you'll notice the faces are again disjointed but only arranged nicer this time. You can also confirm by hovering over a square and pressing *L* or alternatively, selecting a vertice and pressing *Ctrl+L* (Menu version: *Select → Select Linked*).

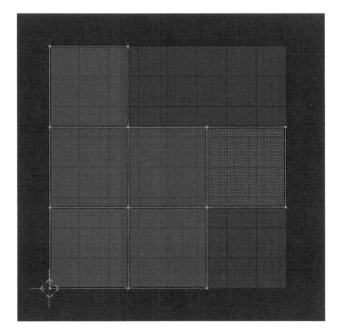

(9) Although it is nice, we generally don't want so many separate islands of squares on our UV map. Imagine having to texture a complex 3D model like a character. We don't want a bunch of disjointed faces that are arranged anywhere. We want them connected nicely since it would be nicer to texture. So let's strategically place seams so that it unwraps nicely. To do this, select the bottom face of the cube only and then *Ctrl+E -> Clear Seam*. This will remove the seams you created on this face.

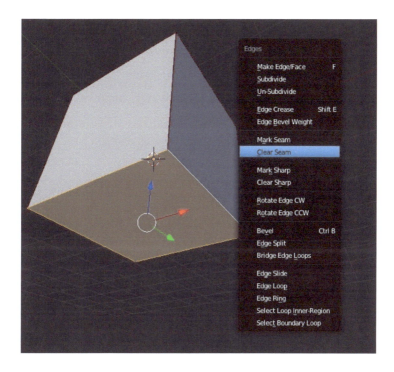

(10) On the top face of the cube, select any one edge. Then *Ctrl+E -> Clear Seam*.

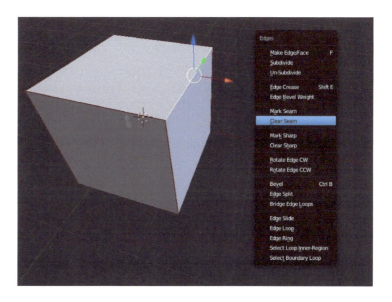

(11)   Now do **U -> Unwrap** again. You should see a cube nicely unfolded and ready to have textures on them. The placement of the seams was really just trial and error. You need to have a good eye for selecting seams as it would improve your skills as a texturer (if that's a word). Complex 3D models require good placement of seams, like characters for example.

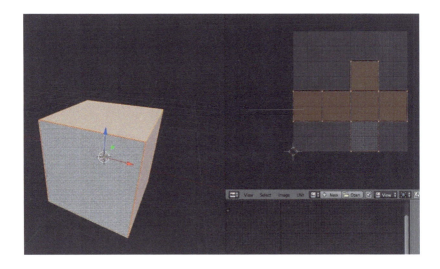

Texture time!

It is now time to texture and see how our UV map affects our 3D model. If you don't know anything about Blender Shaders, see this tutorial!

(12)   To add an image texture, add a new material (Press "Use Nodes" if a material is already there) and then in the Node Editor, add an *Image Texture* by doing **Shift+A -> Texture -> Image Texture** and connect it to the *Diffuse Shader*. Below is what you should have.

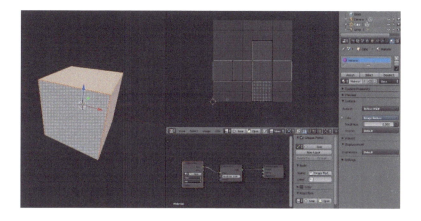

(13) Load an image in the Image Texture node and then go back to the *UV/Image Editor* and open up the image you loaded in. You don't have to open up the directory again to find your image as it should already be loaded in when you opened in the Image Texture node. Just click the image file icon with the up/down arrow (next to the UVs menu option) and select your image.

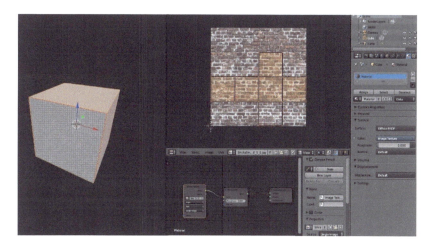

(14) In the 3D viewport, change the viewport type to *Material* or *Texture* (whichever you like).

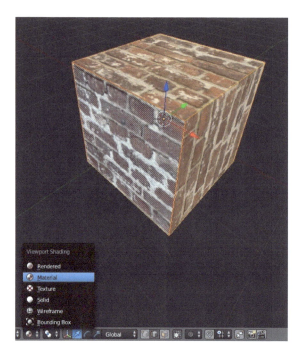

(15) Select all vertices in the *UV/Image editor* by pressing *A* and then move/rotate/scale them anywhere (by pressing *G*, *R* and *S* respectively).

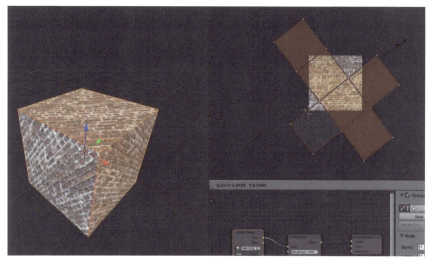

(16) Observe the change in the 3D viewport. You can see that the image texture is also being overlayed over your 3D model.

This is how you control the exact position. This is how you put that tattoo on that bad dude's arm.

Summary

I hope I have demystified the process of Blender UV mapping for you! It really isn't all that hard. The main challenge is selecting the best places to put those seams and transforming the map around the image till it looks good on the 3D model. Luckily there are tutorials out there on the Internet to help you do that and I suggest you follow them. Try also playing around with the other types of UV mapping like *Project from View* and see how that changes the look of your 3D models. In the next chapter, we will focus on lighting! Lighting is the key to any good render as it does not only serve to make our 3D world merely visible but can also set things like the tone, mood, location, or perhaps, more obviously, time of day.

CHAPTER EIGHT

Lighting

In this chapter, you will learn about the basic lights that are available in Blender and some basic (and good looking) lighting setups you can use in your own scenes straight away.

Using Blender Cycles, you can create some awesome looking lighting for your scenes. Especially with Cycles, you can light up your scenes quite professionally with a simple setup in minutes. A few years ago, back in the days of Blender Internal, you would have to spend some times to build a complicated looking lighting setup to light up something as simple as a room. Nowadays, it's a lot simpler and if you're a beginner, you will find lighting your scenes in Blender to be quite intuitive. In this beginner, Blender lighting tutorial, you will learn about using Blender's lights in no time!

Lighting Types in Blender

But first, we must know about the different types of lights you have at your disposal. In your 3D viewport, you can add lights in a similar way to adding meshes. That is, by pressing *Shift+A → Lamp*.

- *Point:* This light shines from the point source in all directions. The light travels some distance before it dies off. This light would be ideal for desk lamps, ceiling lights, or any other item where there is a definite light source.

- *Sun:* This light shines with uniform strength everywhere. It never dies off no matter how further away it is from your scene. Thus, changing the location of the sun lamp does nothing. Rotating the sun lamp however, would change the direction of the sun light. This is obviously a great lamp to simulate the sunlight of a bright sunny day or a nice evening.

- *Spot:* Behaves like a spot light. You rotate the light in the direction where you want to cast the spot light. Currently, with Cycles, you won't see the halo effect god ray thingy when you shine your spot light on something. You would have to set up volumetrics to make the god rays appear.

- *Hemi:* Shines light 180 degrees and, like the sunlight, can be positioned anywhere without changing the lighting and can be rotated to change the direction. This light is great for fill lights or to simulate light from the blue sky.

- *Area:* Area lights also cast light from a point (like a Point lamp) except the light source is larger and in the shape of a square/rectangle. Because of the larger size, these lights tend to give softer shadows. Great for studio photography type shots and shopping mall lights!

- *Emission mesh:* Although not an actual lamp in Blender, Cycles has a material shader type called "Emission". This means your meshes can also emit light! Pretty cool! Obviously, you could do tons of stuff with this, like make some fireworks or create a god-like character which emits light, or campfires or even create that glowy fish from Finding Nemo.

A little note about lights: If you want to do stuff with lights such as change color or strength, you need to select your lamp and then go to the *Object Data* tab in the Property panel. Figure 11 below shows me changing color and strength of the lamps. You might see a thing you can change called 'size'. This means how large your light is. Large sizes means your light is larger and thus gives you softer shadows. Smaller sizes means your light source is tiny and will thus give you sharper shadows.

Basic Lighting Setups

Although this isn't really Blender-related, here are some basic and decent lighting setups you can use in your scenes to make your scene awesome times better.

3-point lighting setup: This lighting setup is mainly for studio photography type shots. To simulate this, you need 3 lamps. They can all be either Area lamps or plane meshes with Emission shaders as materials.

The 3 lamps are called Key Light, Fill Light and Back Light. The Key Light is pretty much the main light that shines on your subject. The Fill Light compliments the Key Light and shines from a side angle. The Back Light shines from the back of the subject to give it that nice silhouette look. Explaining this in detail would be a tutorial on its own. Click here to learn from the masters!

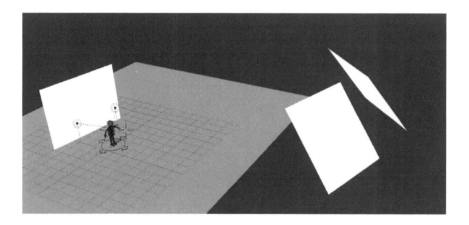

Daytime Light setup: This is a simple setup but might not be obvious to the newbie. To simulate daytime, all you need is a sun lamp with high strength (say 8 with size 0.001) and a hemi lamp with low strength (say 1). The sun lamp should be a yellowy color and the hemi lamp should be a light blue color. If you want an evening sunlight, change the sun color to orange and use a larger size like 0.008 or something. This will give you those softer shadows you see in evening sunlight. Nowadays though, the trend seems to be HDR lighting. Again a tutorial on its own, but you would load a sky HDR image in the World properties panel and set the strength to however much you feel is required. This is shown below but I don't use a HDR image, I just use a plain blue sky color.

NOTE: HDR images use a lot of memory so be sure to use it only if you want epic photorealism.

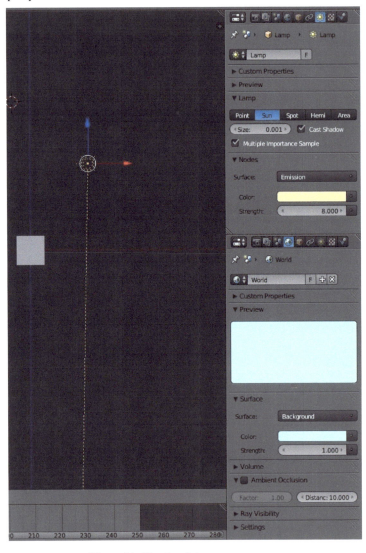

Figure 11. Daytime light setup

Indoor Light setup: This is one of the more difficult light setups to get right in Cycles. It seems no matter what I do, I always get TONS of noise from interior rendering in Cycles. Anyway, a typical light setup would involve a sun lamp angled to shine through a window, and area lamps that fit the size of the window. The Sun Lamp would have a yellowy color and a high strength (say 8 with size 0.001) and Area Lamps with low strength with blue-ish color, like the sky.

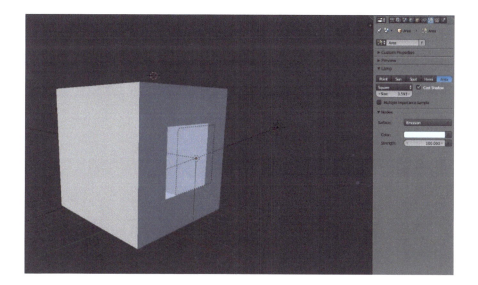

Summary

In this chapter, you looked at the different types of lights Blender has to offer as well as some basic lighting setups you could use in your own scenes to give nice looking results. In the next chapter, we start to learn a bit about sculpting in Blender. This is useful for creating high-detailed kind of stuff like a wrinkly elderly person, dinosaurs or fantasy creatures.

CHAPTER NINE

Sculpting

In this chapter, you will learn about the basics of sculpting! While you won't learn how to make highly detailed monsters or terrains, you will learn a bit about the tools used to make them. Creating awesome, epic and highly detailed works only comes with practice and practice. We will only lay the foundations in this chapter so that you can go away and try it out and become familiar with sculpting in Blender.

Have you ever wondered how these detailed looking renders were made? All those wrinkles, pores and veins? Well, I guess normal and displacement maps can be good at that kind of stuff but for more higher-end awesomeness, you can achieve this look with sculpting! Sculpting can give even better looking detailed renders compared to modeling by hand or relying on bump maps. With the latest developments in Blender, such as dynamic topology, you now have the ability to model a complete detailed character via sculpting by starting with just a cube. Let's take a look at how we can sculpt in Blender.

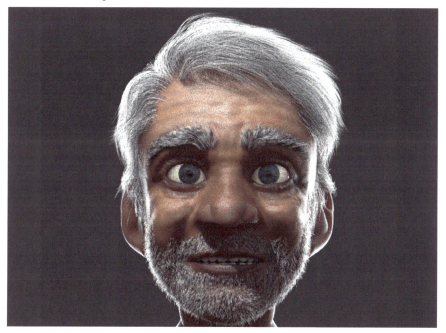

Figure 12. A character made from sculpting for my film "Uyir"

Sculpting in Blender

(1) First things first, open up Blender. We'll use the cube so delete the lamp and camera if you want.

(2) Of course, you can't do much sculpting on a cube since it only has 8 vertices. If you want to do high detail sculpting, you'll need much more than 8 vertices (think 100s to 1000s). So, all you have to do is just add a *Multires* modifier on the cube. We can't use the *Subsurf* modifier when sculpting for some reason. The *Multires* does pretty much the same thing anyway.

(3) Bump up the *Multires* to about 4 or so. Won't give us 100s of vertices but is good enough. The higher the value, the more you can detail your cube (should now look like a sphere) but obviously the higher you push this value, the more you're going to strain your computer's processors. I have crashed my computer oh-so many times doing this.

(4) Next, with the cube selected, go into *Sculpt mode*.

(5) You should see a bunch of sculpting-related goodness in the Toolbar on the left. Here you can choose different paint brushes and stuff. There are all sorts of cool brushes you can use. For example, the *Draw* brush allows you to draw on your mesh (cool for drawing veins), the *Smooth* brush will smooth your mesh, and so on. Pretend as if your mesh is one of those clays you used to play with in school, and the brushes as one of the tools you can use to shape your clay.

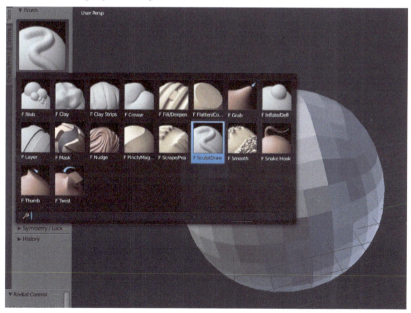

(6) There are a bunch of options you can play with in the brush settings. You will likely see Add/Subtract buttons on a lot of the brushes. The *Add* button bumps up your mesh as your draw and the *Subtract* button carves into your mesh as you draw (cool for drawing wrinkles).

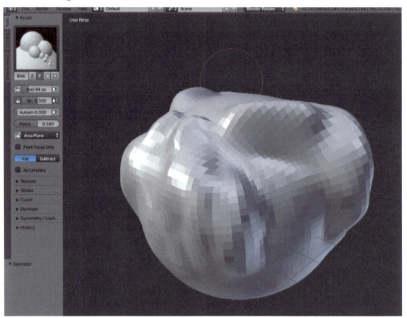

Dynamic sculpting in Blender

Blender has a pretty awesome feature called *DynaTopo* which means Dynamic Topology. This means that when you use the brushes on your mesh, the mesh will dynamically create vertices for you as you draw. You don't need to rely on *Multires*. The good thing about this is that you save a lot of memory, since a dynamic sculpt will only focus on adding a lot of vertices around wherever the detail is required whereas a *Multires* will add a lot of vertices all over which is just unnecessary and CPU-hogging. The bad thing about *DynaTopo*, however, is that you won't end up having a nice topology structure once you've sculpted. Vertices will be placed randomly here and there and it will just be a mess. Certainly a nightmare to animate with! But there is a way to fix this using a technique called Re-topology, but that is a more advanced topic.

To enable dynamic topology in Blender, just go to the toolbar and under Options, you should see a check box with something like *"Enable Dynamic Topology"* depending on what Blender version you use. Click to enable and you can dynamically start creating a full detailed character starting from a cube! Oh yeah, make sure you remove the *Multires* modifier, it is not needed anymore, we have *DynaTopo* now.

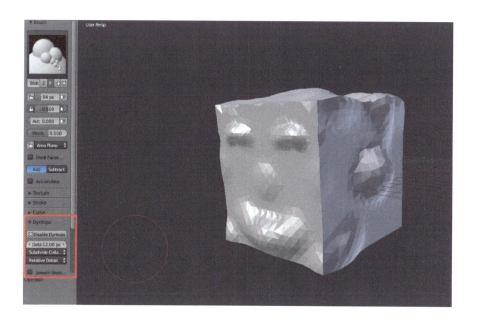

Summary

In this chapter, we learnt about how to sculpt in Blender and a bit about dynamic topology. If you find yourself developing a passion for sculpting, I highly encourage you to check out some of the videos on YouTube where artists show timelapses of their sculpting. I find it to be quite enjoyable and you can learn some new techniques and skills just from watching those masters in action! In the next chapter, you will learn about getting started with animation in Blender. You will finally get things moving around and doing stuff!

CHAPTER TEN

Animation

In this chapter, we will learn how to get started with animation in Blender! We will also animate a ball just simply moving. By the end of this chapter, you will know the ways to animate in Blender and the types of properties you can animate as well!

Animation in Blender is very quick and easy. If you want to make a box move from point A to another point B in 3 seconds, all you have to do is move the box to point A on frame 0 and then set a 'key' (also known as keyframing). 3 seconds down the timeline, move the box to point B and then set another 'key'. When you play back the animation, you will see your box move from point A to point B in 3 seconds. Simple as that! You've made you're first animation.

You can do a lot more than that, though! You can animate how it rotates, as well as how big or small it scales. All you have to do is set keys anytime you want something to happen. A key (or keyframe) pretty much just sets (or "locks") the properties of the object at that specific time. So say, I set a keyframe on the 5th second of a cube that is rotated 30 degrees, that is located 5 units above the Z-axis and scaled 2 times the original. That means, when I playback the animation, the cube will always be rotated 30 degrees, and be located 5 units above the Z-axis and be scaled twice the original size when the playback has passed the 5th second. By setting a key, we have 'locked' our object with those properties in place. Here is a tutorial that covers keyframing better in case I explained it horribly! I guess it's nice to know that Blender can do all of this, but exactly HOW do you do all this?!?

Ways to Animate in Blender

There are 2 different ways you can animate in Blender:

Pressing the i key

To set a key (or keyframe) in Blender, you simply press the *i* key on your keyboard. You may be presented with a number of options. Depending on whether you want to animate the *location* only, *rotation* only, *scale* only, or a combination of the others, then you select the option that corresponds. Suppose you will regularly need to animate *location*, *rotation* and *scale* all at once. You would then select 'LocRotScale'. This would set keys for the *location*, *rotation* and *scale* properties of the object. If you're a serial animator and you hate having to select an option every time you press *i*, you can set the Active Keying Set (found in the bottom of the Timeline next to the red circled button) to LocRotScale. Just press that key looking image inside the textbox and you'll find those options. Now every time you want to animate your object, you simply press *i* without having a dropdown option to annoy you!

Automatic keyframe insertion

Another way to animate in Blender (and a personal favorite of mine!) is to use the automatic keyframe insertion! This is that red-circled button I mentioned earlier (which looks like a video camera record button) found in the Timeline. Once clicked, it will assume you are animating with the option LocRotScale. If you want to change this to something else, change the Active Keying Set (the box next to it) to another option that you prefer. To set a keyframe, you simply work with your object directly. Say you move an object to point A, a keyframe should already be set (you should see a yellow line indicating a key in the Timeline). If you go to another point in the timeline, and move somewhere else, another keyframe would automatically be inserted. Blender detects any change in the objects properties and sets a key if a property has changed.

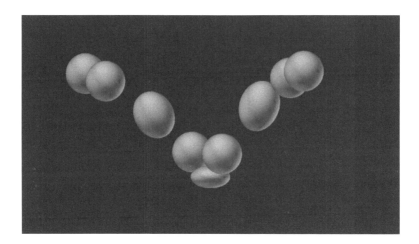

Give it a go for yourself!

Here's a quick little exercise to try out if it's your first time doing animation in Blender.

(1) Start with a *UV sphere*.

(2) At frame 1, set a keyframe (using *i* or *automatic keyframe insertion*).

(3) Then go to frame 10.

(4) Move the sphere somewhere else and add another keyframe.

(5) Playback your animation (by pressing the *play* button or *Alt+A*).

(6) Congratulations on your first animation in Blender!

Properties

Just a quick little note about properties in Blender. You saw that when you animate an object in Blender, you set keys for the location, rotation and scale. These are properties in Blender. A key is set for the location property, rotation property and scale property. You are not limited to this only. Almost **every** property in Blender can be animated! You can animate the Depth of Field settings for your camera. For your shader, you can animate the strength of the *Emission shader* or even animate the changing of color in the *Diffuse shader*. You can animate the turning on and off of lights and even light color changes. You can animate your sky to change from morning to afternoon to sunset to night. The list just goes on and on!

To try this out for yourself, go to a property (for example, the Lamp strength property which is found in the lamp's *Object Data* tab in the Properties window). Then, hover your mouse over the strength and press *i*. You can go to another frame in the timeline, change the strength and press *i* again. If you render out an animation, you will see the light dim or strengthen depending on the values you keyed in.

Summary

That's all you need to know for now! In this chapter, you have learnt the 2 ways of animating objects and the types of properties you can animate (such as location, rotation and scale). Of course, there are more advanced types of animations you can do in Blender such as armature animation (that is, animating characters and so on) but that is best left for another day. Same principles still apply though, you use either the *i* key or *automatic keyframe insertion* to animate your characters. Give it a go, animate something cool. Download or make a quick car 3D model and animate it driving around a race track. With a bit more practice, you will get used to Blender's animation system. In the next chapter, we will look at working with particles in Blender. This is great for fireworks, rain, hair and fur. You will learn to make your own particles and play around with making them look the way you want!

CHAPTER ELEVEN

The Particle System

In this chapter, we will learn about working with particles in Blender to create cool looking effects! By the end of this chapter, you will have a better understanding of how the Particle System in Blender works as well as have a basic knowledge of creating particle streams and hair/fur.

If you've watched some 3D animated flicks, you may have wondered how they create fireworks, rain, glowing orbs, dust particles or even hair/fur. The secret all lies in particles! In Blender, we use the in-built particle system to re-create these effects. So let's take a look at how to use this system!

Figure 13. Hair/Fur and Grass created with Particle System in Blender for "Big Buck Bunny"

Using Blender's particle system

Let's play around with the Particle System in Blender for quite a bit and observe the effects. You will learn a bit about the Particle System this way.

(1) Delete everything and leave the cube. Select the cube.

(2) Select the *Particles* tab in the Properties window.

(3) Press the 'New' button to create a new particle system for the cube. Now playback your animation (*Alt+A*) and you should see that your box is now emitting particles. Your cube should sort of act like the nozzle of a shower head.

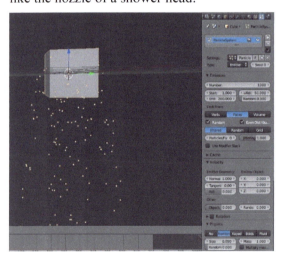

(4) This is made possible by the bunch of default settings that have been automatically set up for you when you created a new particle system. Play around with these settings to make the particles do weird stuff.

(5) A few things. The *Emission* bit of the settings are used to control how many particles you want, the start time for when the particles for when the particles should appear and the end time for when they should go away. The *Physics* bit controls how the particles move and their sizes and other physical related stuff. The *Cache* is used to store your final particle animation either in a separate file or within the blend file. This is highly recommended if you are happy with the final animation of the particles since when you want to render or preview later on, it would not have to re-calculate the animation.

(6) If you don't want gravity to affect its movement, you can switch off the gravity completely. Either go to the scene tab and change the Gravity Z-setting from -9.81 to 0. This will affect the gravity of your whole scene. So if any object relies on gravity, they too will be affected. Another (better) way is to turn off the gravity for just the emitting cube. In the Particle tabs, you will see a section called Field Weights. Here, slide the gravity to 0.

(7) By playing around with these settings, you will be able to simulate fireworks or rain or even floating dust particles.

Let's create hair

The particle system is not only used to simulate fireworks and stuff, you can also make hair and fur using it. Here's how to do that:

(1) Change the *Type* from 'Emitter' to 'Hair' in the *Particle* settings, you would notice your particle system now becomes your hair system.

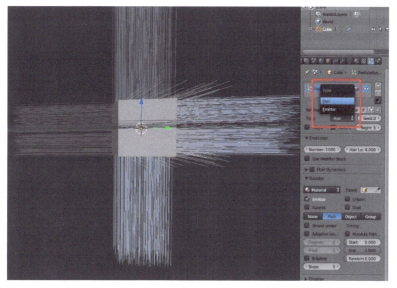

(2) Play with the settings for a bit. Similar to the emitter, changing the *Emission* number will change how many strands of hair your mesh will have. That is, bumping up the *Emission* number to 2000 will give your cube 2000 hair strands.

(3) Let's comb that hair! At the moment, it looks like the cube has suffered an electric shock or something. So we should comb that hair back into place. In the 3D view, switch from *Object Mode* to *Particle Edit*.

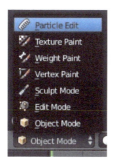

(4) Just like sculpting, you will see a bunch of brush options in the toolbar on the left (press **T** to open if you don't see it). Select the *Comb* brush.

(5) You are now the barber! Go to your mesh and ***left-click drag*** to start combing. Go crazy and comb that unruly hair to any shape you want.

(6) You might find that your mesh has WAY too much hair everywhere and it probably needs trimming. Well, you are the barber here and you have full control over how you want your hair to look. Select the *Cut* brush and cut away at the hairs you don't want. If you want to trim hair and not cut it off completely, make sure you cut along the outer edges.

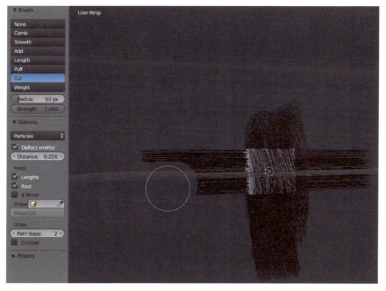

(7) Just a final thing that might help beginners as this part might confuse.

NOTE: This applies to those using older versions of Blender (before 2.76). If you want to give your hair a shader, go to the *Particle* Settings, under *Render* choose **Material: 2**. Now in the material settings, create a new material under the already existing material 'Material'. This new material will be the hair's material. Why? When you selected Material: 2, you actually mean the second material of the mesh. So if you had like 5 materials for your mesh in total, and you selected 'Material: 4' in the particle settings, the hair will render with the 4th material in the slot. A little confusing but that is currently how Blender works. In the future, this might change and this post might become redundant, but for now it is just the way it is.

If you are using a new version of Blender (mine is around Blender 2.76), you will still need to create a new material under the existing 'Material'. Then in the *Particle* settings, under *Render*, change the material from the dropdown directly! Easy as that!

Other uses of the Particle System

I have to mention that the hair system is not ONLY used to make hair and fur. You can replace those hair strands with 3D models (which is done by going to the ***Particle Settings → Render → Change to Object → Select your object***). This means you aren't just limited to hair but you can create forests of trees, cities, crowds of people, flock of birds, you name it. The particle system saves a lot of memory so rendering 1000s of trees will not break your PC compared to you duplicating a tree 1000s of times and rendering that. The image below was created by me where I used tree models to represent hair strands!

Figure 14. My dodgy attempt at creating an aerial island forest

Summary

In this chapter, you learned about working with particles in Blender and have a better understanding of how artists may use the Particle System to create effects like hair/fur, fireworks and dust. If you're interested in doing cool stuff with particles, I highly advise you to keep playing around with the particle settings and observing the results. Or even follow some online tutorials. You can make all sorts of cool stuff with particles! In the next chapter, we look at the Physics system in Blender. So now we get to learn about making our 3D objects interact and do things according to the laws of Physics. Don't worry, you don't need to be a Physics expert to learn about this (although it doesn't hurt to know at least a little bit!).

CHAPTER TWELVE

The Physics System

In this chapter, you will learn about getting started with using the Physics System in Blender! By the end of this chapter, you will have better knowledge of how to do basic physics in Blender which will lay the foundation of doing more advanced stuff later on your own.

Working with physics in Blender is really quite easy. You will be able to make some cool physics simulations in Blender and best of all, you don't really need to be that good at Physics (although it does help if you are!).

First, let's take a look at how you would simulate physics in Blender.

With a cube selected, if you go to the last tab of the Properties window, you will see a Physics tab. This is where you go if you need to set up physics. Note that this isn't the only way to create physics in Blender. You can do it via modifiers or if you via some plugins if you enable them. But by default, if you want to create a simulated bouncing of a ball or collisions, or cloth movement, you would go to the Physics tab.

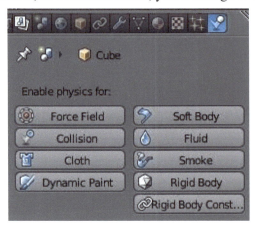

Simple as that! As you can see from the different options in the tab above, you can create all sorts of cool physics.

Some of these buttons should be quite self-explanatory in what they do. But I'll give a brief explanation of what each of these do anyway:

- **Force Field:** Your selected object will behave as a force field. This can be useful if you want to recreate that scene where Moses parts the Red Sea.
- **Collision:** Your selected object will behave as a collision object. Other objects that have physics on them will not be able to penetrate through your object and will instead bounce off it.
- **Cloth:** Your selected object will act like cloth. Best to use this on cloth meshes.
- **Dynamic Paint:** Mostly needed for textures that need to

update in real time dynamically. Some examples include creating rain drop textures on a roadway as it rains. Or a wall being dynamically painted as a painter paints away.

- **Soft Body:** Your selected object will behave as a soft body. That is a blobby, gooey kind of thing. That was a poor explanation but it was the best way I could describe it. Use this for things like jelly or custard objects.

- **Fluid:** Used to simulate fluid or liquid. This is best used to simulate a glass of water, or water in a fishbowl, or even an ocean. Anything that involves liquids.

- **Smoke:** Used to simulate smoke and fire. This is best used to simulate fire in a burning building. It can also simulate a calm and peaceful campfire, or even massive and deadly nuclear explosions. You can get awesome and realistic looking results from this.

- **Rigid Body/Rigid Body Constraints:** This is used for all sorts of cool physics-related stuff. For example, you can make a stack of cards fall over each other, or simulate a car crash. You can simulate a jar being filled with marbles. You can also make things fall and bounce and collide with each other. This is a popular tool that is used by Blender users and you can see some of the cool stuff the Blender community has made with this all over the Internet.

It might be a little overkill if I go through each of these physics simulations and explain the settings one-by-one. Especially as a complete beginner, it might be a little too much to take in if you're just starting out. So let's take it easy and start off with a really simple example: A colliding ball.

The Colliding ball

To make our colliding ball simulation, we're going to be using the Rigid Body tools in the Physics panel.

(1) Start off by first deleting everything and adding a plane (Make sure the cursor is in the center, if not just do **Shift+S** → **Cursor to Center**). Scale it to be big enough.

(2) Go to the *Physics* tab and click "Rigid Body". Then, set the type to "Passive". This will make it a collision object and won't move when played back.

(3) Add a Suzanne monkey (**Shift+A** → **Mesh** → **Monkey**) and also set a Rigid body with type "Passive". Move the monkey up a bit (**G** →**Z** →**1**).

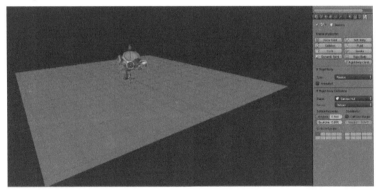

(4) Now add a sphere, which will act as our ball. Move it up past the monkey (**G** →**Z** →**5**).

(5) Give it a Rigid body but keep the type as "Active". This will allow the ball to move according to the simulation.

(6) Playback your animation (*Alt+A*) and observe your colliding ball.

(7) Pretty cool! Add more "Passive" objects here and there and see your ball react to it. You could add more "Active" objects as well and see how they react.

That's pretty much a part of how the Blender physics system works! There's more you can do with Blender physics however, but is too much to cover in one chapter and probably requires a dedicated book on its own!

Summary

In this chapter, you've learnt the bare basics of the Physics System in Blender. Just keep playing around with the Blender physics system and very soon you will be comfortable making your own epic simulations. In the next chapter, we will look at rendering in Blender. In other words, making sure your output renders look as good as possible!

CHAPTER THIRTEEN

Rendering

In this chapter, you will learn how to render stills or animations in Blender! We will cover some of the basic settings needed to make your renders look the way you want it. By the end of this chapter, you will have a better understanding of how to render as effectively and efficiently as possible in Blender.

Rendering in Blender is very easy. If you want to render a still, press the *Render* button in the Render panel or just press the **F12** key. Then when it's rendered, you can save the image by opening **Image -> Save as Image** in the *UV/Image editor* window.

If you want to render an animation, press the *Animation* button or alternatively, press **Shift+F12**.

But, before you render anything out, you'd probably want to tweak a few settings to make sure your renders output the way **you** want it!

So here is the Render panel:

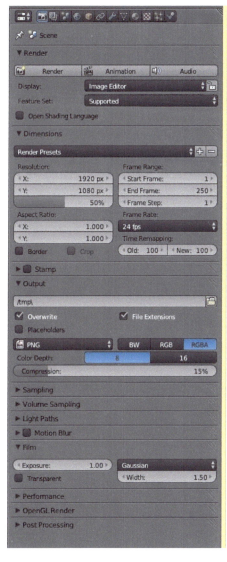

(Yours might look a little different depending on what Blender version you have.)

The Dimensions settings is where you can set things like the final resolution of your render. For example, if you want HD resolution, you would set 1920×1080. Just below that, where you see the 50%, determines the percentage of the resolution that will render. So with 1920×1080 with 50%, it will render an image/animation that is 0.5 HD. The point of this percentage is for you to quickly create test renders without having to mess up your final render settings. You can also set things like the start and end frame, the frame rate of your animation and so on.

If you render an animation, you need to set where the output will be stored. In the Render settings, under Output, this is where you set where you want your animation to be stored. You can also change the output type. If you leave it at the default PNG, it will render a series of PNG images in the output folder you selected. There are other different output types such as Xvid, H.264, MPEF, JPG, etc. Here's what I usually do for my animations: When you render animations in Blender, it's best to render to a series of images than a video clip. Why? Because if Blender crashes while in the middle of rendering a video clip, I have an incomplete video clip. Whereas with image sequences, if Blender crashes, I just reload and continue from the frame where Blender crashes. So I would choose something like PNG or JPG. Later on, once everything is rendered, I combine these images to a video clip (for which I then choose H.264).

Figure 15. High samples vs Low Samples

This is an important one: **Sampling**! Setting a higher sample value will give you less "noise" in your renders but will take longer to render. Less samples are obviously quicker with more "noise". It's best to find a compromise between the two. If you're rendering a still image, then time shouldn't really be a factor and you can get away with more samples. Render times are generally more important for animations and if you're willing to wait that bit longer for an epic scene, then you can use larger samples. It's all about compromise! Just below that setting is Preview samples. You can set how many samples you want to use for Preview purposes. This generally should be lower than the final full samples. To actually see the preview renders, you'd go to the 3D viewport, and change the *Viewport Shading* type from the default 'Solid' to 'Rendered'.

Just in case I confused you, Preview renders show how your world will look when rendered in real time! This is the cool thing about the Cycles render engine. You can visualise in real-time what your scene looks like with all the materials and the lighting all calculated in real time. You can get faster previews using your GPU instead of your CPU. GPU can also speed up your renders MUCH faster than your CPU. To change to GPU rendering, all you need to do is go to *User Preferences* → *System tab* → *Compute device* → *Change to CUDA* (or whatever your GPU is) and select your GPU.

Another important setting is Performance. Under performance, you can set things like how many threads you want to render with. If you have one of those powerful Intel Quad-Core Processors, you will have 8 threads available to you. That is, your renders will be 8 times faster than using 1 thread. The more threads you have, the better. Auto-detect will automatically detect how much threads you can use. Personally, I always manually set fixed number of threads to 1 less than my maximum. This is so that I can work on something else while my epic film is being crunched. When I use all threads, I find that my PC becomes slow and laggy to work with.

Summary

That's the end of this chapter! You now have an idea how to render stills and animations and settings you need to make your scene look as good as possible without wasting time (as well as breaking your PC). These settings are all that is needed to configure your renders. Depending on what settings you choose, setting up for higher quality will usually slow down render times and setting up for fast render times will compromise some quality. In the next chapter, we will look at using Blender as a video editor. Something to replace Windows Movie Maker!

CHAPTER FOURTEEN

Blender as a Video Editor

In this chapter, you will learn about using Blender as a video editor! While you might not abandon Windows Movie Maker anytime soon, you will still see the potential of using Blender as a pretty useful video editor. By the end of this chapter, you will know the basics of video editing in Blender.

You might have worked with other video editors such as Windows Movie Maker, or Cyberlink PowerDirector or even other higher end video editing software like Premiere. While Blender isn't primarily known to be a competent video editor, it still is quite powerful. In fact, my own films "Uyir", "Vetri" and "Tripping" were all edited within Blender!

So how do we use Blender as a video editor?

The Video Sequence Editor (VSE)

In Blender, all you need to do is change the screen layout from 'Default' to 'Video Editing' (likely the last one in the list). This gives you a new layout of Blender that mimics a professional video editor.

Working with Video

To import video or image sequences, go to the Video Sequence Editor window and press *Add* → *Movie* (for movie clips) or *Add* → *Image* (for an image or image sequences). You then proceed to select your clip or image. For image sequences, go to the folder where you have your image sequence and then press *A*. This will select all the images in the folder. You can also do box select by pressing *B* and left-click dragging (*middle-click dragging* will de-select). Once you have selected your sequence and pressed *Add Image Strip*, you will see your new strip in the editor. The same goes for a movie clip. We call these "strips".

You can work with these strips and do whatever you like with them. Just like when modeling, you can move them around by pressing **G**. You can hide them by pressing **H** and unhide by **Alt+H**. You can duplicate a strip by pressing **Shift+D**. You can also cut a strip in half. You do this by left-clicking anywhere near the middle of the strip (this moves the current frame to where you clicked). Then press **K**. The cut should be made. You will have 2 different strips to work with. To delete a strip, you just press **X** → **Erase** strips.

You can overlay a strip on top of another strip. You can create a nice fade effect or transition effect by animating the "Opacity" value on the right. You will be able to see a preview in the top right part of the screen.

If you want to trim a video strip, you can right-click on the edges of the strip where you see the arrow to select and move (by pressing **G**). You can then trim up to where you want. Right-clicking in the middle of the strip will select the whole strip, and right-clicking the sides where the arrows are, will select the handles to trim.

Working with Audio

You can also throw in audio files as well. Most common formats will work well. Sometimes you might find that there will be a syncing problem with the video and audio in Blender. That's because Blender might not be fast enough to catch up the video playback with the audio. You can fix this at the bottom where you see "No Sync" to "AV-sync". This will drop some frames from playback so that it matches the audio. Great for dialogue scenes where lip syncing is important.

Creating cool effects

You can create some cool effects with Blender. In the VSE, select a strip and if you go to **Add → Effect Strip**, you will see a bunch of effects that you have at your disposal. For example, if you choose Speed Control, you can control how fast or slow your video goes. You can create a slow-motion effect yourself. You can control how fast or slow you want your video to go by selecting one of the side arrows on the speed control strip and moving it out or in. This will automatically slow down or speed up the strip to fit the new length.

Sometimes you might be happy with how 2 strips are interacting with each other and combine them into 1 strip. You do this by pressing **Ctrl+G → Make Meta Strip**.

The Output

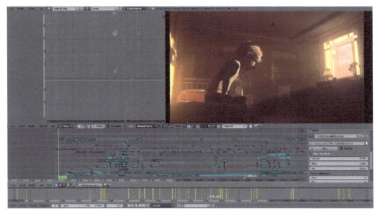

Figure 16. The final edit for my short animated film "Uyir"

Once the video editing is all done, you can render it out. Just change the screen layout back from 'Video Editing' to 'Default'. Then change the rendering settings as appropriate. The settings I usually use is 1920×1080 (100%), H.264 video, MP3 audio with 192kbps. You don't need to mess with sampling or anything like that, the video editing sequence doesn't care about that. Choose an output folder and give your video a cool name under the *Output* settings. When ready, press the *Animation* button (or *Ctrl+F12*). Wait, go outside and smell the fresh air, and then come back to see your video masterpiece all ready to be uploaded to Youtube or shown to family/friends.

Summary

In this chapter, you learned about using Blender as a Video Editor! Blender's video editor isn't the best in the world but it does get the job done. There's actually a lot more advanced stuff you can do with Blender's video editor, too much to fit into one chapter. I plan to dedicate a few posts on my blog about using Blender as a video editor so be sure to check them out if you are interested! In the next chapter, we will end the book by delving into a bit of compositing. That is, giving your renders that final pop and converting your renders from looking 100% to 120%.

CHAPTER FIFTEEN

The Compositor

In this chapter, you will learn how to do some basic compositing in Blender! In other words, you will learn how to create effects and filters on your rendered images to make it look even better. By the end of this chapter, you will have a basic understanding of what it takes to make your rendered images look really awesome.

As we reach the final chapter of this book, I thought I would give a brief introduction to the Blender compositor! I mainly use the compositor to take my renders to the next level. If I find my renders to be 100% good looking, using the compositor sometimes pops it up to 110-120%. We use the compositor to add that final pop to our image. We make our CG-looking renders stand out and come alive.

The compositor can be used to give your scenes a different mood. By changing a few settings in the compositor, you can make your scene look happy and cheerful to moody and menacing. With the compositor, you can do a TON of things like add glow effects, lens flares, vignettes, professional color-grading, DoF (Depth of Field), misty effects, light leaks, chromatic aberrations and so on. It really is quite powerful and what I always use on my own films. I don't think I've ever released any work without some form of compositing applied.

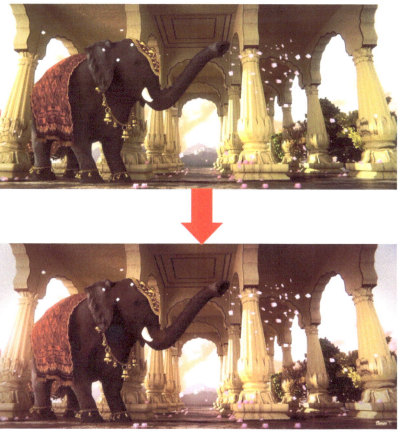

Figure 17.Here's a render before compositing and after compositing

How compositing works

Compositing is basically a bunch of nodes working together to give you a nicer image (that's not the dictionary meaning, just my own interpretation). To put simply, you have a node containing your render. You then plug in a bunch of nodes. Say a node that makes an image brighter, another node that makes an image glow, and so on. When you connect the image node to the input of the image brightening node, the result or output from the image brightening node, is the original image that is now brighter. Then when you connect the output of the image brightening node to the input of the glow node, the output of the glow node is a brightened image that now glows. I hope that made sense.

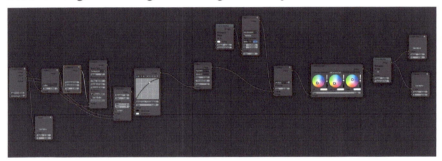

Make an image brighter.

Perhaps working by example will help. So here are the steps to start working with compositing in Blender:

(1) Change the layout from 'Default' to 'Compositing'.

(2) Enable 'Use Nodes', 'Free Unused Nodes' and 'Backdrop'.

(3) There's not much compositing you can do with a grey cube on a grey background, so let's use an image instead. Select the *Render Layers* node by ***right-clicking*** the node. Then press *X*.

(4) Add an *Image* node (***Shift+A*** ➔ *Input* ➔ *Image*). Press

Open on the node and select an image that you have. You can use any image of your own choosing.

(5) Now connect the output of the image node to the Image input of the Compositing node. You do this by **left-click dragging** from the output of the *Image* node and letting go of the mouse when you reach the input of *Compositing* node. This means your image will now be rendered as is.

(6) Now add a *Viewer* node so that we can see our change as we are working. Press **Shift+A → Output → Viewer**.

(7) Similarly like you did to the *Compositing* node, connect the output of the *Image* node to the image input of the *Viewer* node. You should immediately see your image as a background.

(8) Let's make it look brighter! Add a *Bright/Contrast* node by pressing **Shift+A → Color → Bright/Contrast**.

(9) Now let's connect it to the original image. You can do the whole connecting from one input to another but a quick way is to drag the *Bright/Contrast* node (by pressing **G**) and hover it around the middle of the line between the *Image* node and the *Viewer* node. When you see that line turn orange, press **Enter** or **left-click**. You should see the lines automatically re-connect.

(10) Now let's make the image brighter. Turn up the brightness and observe your image change and become brighter.

(11) Note that you can work with the nodes similar to when modeling. For example, duplicate the *Bright/Contrast* node (by pressing **Shift+D**) and place it between the *Viewer* node and the original *Bright/Contrast* node. The result is an even brighter image.

BLENDER 3D FOR BEGINNERS

Summary

And that's compositing! In this chapter, we looked at the benefits of using compositing for our renders. We touched on a bit about nodes and learnt how to make our image brighter. There's a lot more you can do with the compositor. Some of the stuff you could do with the compositor include Depth-Of-Field, motion blur, vignettes and chromatic aberrations to name a few. You will continue to learn about this stuff the more you use Blender. I also encourage you to check out my blog where I cover how to do all this. In the next chapter, we finally conclude the book and recap everything we've learned.

CHAPTER SIXTEEN

Conclusion

In this chapter, we finally recap the main concepts we've learned from this book and finally conclude.

We now recap what we've learned throughout this book below:

- In *Chapter 1*, we provided an introduction to Blender and how to install as well as some inspiration to get you going.
- In *Chapter 2*, we covered the Blender user interface as well as the different windows and screen layouts in Blender.
- In *Chapter 3*, we specifically looked at the Properties window as this is the crux of Blender!
- In *Chapter 4*, we looked at how to navigate our way through Blender and carrying out basic operations on 3D objects.
- In *Chapter 5*, we learnt about the basics of 3D modeling in Blender. We also worked with curves.

- In *Chapter 6*, we covered the different shaders in Blender Cycles render engine. We also created a simple car paint shader.
- In *Chapter 7*, we were introduced to texturing in Blender. We learnt about UV mapping and we unwrapped a cube nicely.
- In *Chapter 8*, we learnt about the different lighting types in Blender and some basic decent-looking lighting setups.
- In *Chapter 9*, we were introduced to sculpting in Blender and touched on dynamic topology.
- In *Chapter 10*, we learnt ways to animate in Blender and the fact that nearly every property in Blender is animate-able!
- In *Chapter 11*, we used the Particle System to simulate particle streams as well as hair/fur.
- In *Chapter 12*, we covered the Physics systems available in Blender and looked at a colliding ball example using the Rigid Body tools.
- In *Chapter 13*, we learnt how to render in Blender, as well as the settings required to get our renders to look the way we want it.
- In *Chapter 14*, we looked at using Blender as a video editor.
- In *Chapter 15*, we covered the compositing system in Blender and how it helps us give awesome looking imagery. We also learnt how to make any image brighter with the compositor in Blender.

That's it!

We've finally come to the end of this book! I hope you enjoyed this book and learnt a lot from it. You are now getting closer to mastering Blender. You are one step closer to making your own epic animated movie or game or whatever it is you plan to use Blender for! The more you actually practice using Blender, the better you will get. I know when I first started out, I didn't give Blender that much love. I even rejected it for a few years before I decided to come back. Persistence really is key and I know you will learn to love Blender better than me because there is just SO MUCH tutorials out there on the Internet right now. It seems like there's a tutorial to do pretty much anything in Blender nowadays.

On my end, I would like to thank you for taking the time to purchasing and reading my book! I completely understand the pain of having to learn Blender and this was one of the reasons why I was motivated to write this book. I wanted to make the process of learning as seamless and as enjoyable to new users as possible. If you felt this book helped you in any way, please leave a short review on Amazon and let me know what you think! I will definitely consider each review and aim to make my upcoming books even better.

About the Author

My name is Danan Thilakanathan and I am a self-taught 3D animator and filmmaker and have been using Blender for about 5 years. I have made 4 animated short films on YouTube using Blender. I started out making animated films and webisodes for YouTube and have now developed a passion to help other people and share the knowledge that I've gained through tutorials. My actual career is nothing related to animation or filmmaking. By day, I am an Engineer and by night, I am a filmmaker. Sometimes, it can be quite challenging to balance both at the same time.

I regularly post tutorials about filmmaking and animation (mostly with Blender) on my blog. If you would like to receive regular updates, please subscribe to the mailing list on my blog. I promise to never spam you with irrelevant stuff. Visit my blog here: http://ThilakanathanStudios.com

Feel free to connect with me on Facebook, Google+ and Tumblr. If you enjoy watching animated videos, then feel free to subscribe to my YouTube channel!

Acknowledgments

First of all, thank you Blender Foundation for providing us with your awesome software Blender for free!

Also, thank you also to the people around me who have been quite motivating and supportive. This have given me motivation to really push through and finish this book!

Thank you so much for reading! Please add a short review on Amazon and let me know what you thought!

If you have a passion for filmmaking and animation, then subscribe to the mailing list on ThilakanathanStudios.com. I will regularly share with you some useful tips and tricks and also beginner Blender tutorials!

Thank you and have fun Blending!
Danan Thilakanathan